Hang Five

Hang Five

Sandy Hiortdahl

Hang Five

Published by bd-studios.com in New York City, 2023
Copyright © 2023 by Sandy Hiortdahl

Photographs from the author's collection
Design by luke kurtis

ISBN 978-1-950231-90-4

"Ahab's Day" originally appeared in *VAYAVYA*, December 2013. "Hanging Five Aboard the Stella Irene" originally appeared in Pen2Paper's 2016 Contest, First Place for Poetry. "Homing Instincts" originally appeared in *Wilderness House Literary Journal*, Summer 2014. "Jokes of Time," originally appeared in *Grasslimb Journal*, Late Summer Issue, 2017. "Ode to Mrs. Hutchinson" originally appeared in *GlassFire Magazine*, Fall 2013. "Yard Circles" originally appeared in *The Summerset Review*, Summer 2014.

All Rights Reserved. No part of this publication may be reproduced, stored in a retrieval system or transmitted in any form or by any means without the prior permission in writing of copyright holders and of the publisher.

For Danny Lane, my one and only,
and also in memory of my parents,
Jack and Stella Hiortdahl

Contents

Rock-a-Bye	9
Hang Five	10
Yellow Time	13
The Flight Sonnets	15
Friday's Child, June 1963	18
Fractions and Bones	26
Jokes of Time	28
Grandmother Minnie	29
Glow Worm Yellow	30
Stowaways	32
Dreamtime Nocturne	39
Because It's Nighttime Again	42
Somewhere in Florida	45
Merging	46
Homing Instincts	51
Weekends at the Longs'	52
Dream Landing	57
Get Your Own	60
Who Cooks for You?	62

Red Bike, Red Keds	64
Green Bike	69
What We No Longer Know	71
Wind Tokens	74
Pop Tops	75
Sideshow, Davidsonville Elementary	76
Learn to Fall	86
Ode to Mrs. Hutchinson	91
Yard Circles	94
Hallowafternoon to E'en	96
Sanctus Peninsula	100
Ahab's Day	102
Two Packs of Kools	107
Dixon Sale on Wednesdays	111
Hand Over Hand	118
Median	120
Bench	125
Nature of Dementia	127
Returning	129
About the Author	135

Rock-a-Bye
Prelude

I notice with relief
the blousy blooms and green
leaves peeking, flouncing
from small limbs.

The relief is not for warmth
as much as safety, as if
we may land gently
in these cushioned arms
if we happen to fall
from the sky—
as if we definitely will fall
from way above and rather
than being speared and sliced
by winter sharp boughs,
we will bounce and sigh
and sleep.

Hang Five
Aboard the Stella Irene

Mother once said I was conceived
on a boat near Solomon's Island,
and so my penchant for all things water,
for dangling my legs over any pier,
bow, stern, or gunwale, one leg freckled,
the other shiny, plastic, fiberglass.

Aboard the *Stella Irene* at age four,
I refused the captain's chair, the offer
to steer, and as we bounced over the waves
I made my way up the starboard beam
to the bow, the wooden boat lively
as some happy puppy heading home.

My father trailed me, caught up, strung
an anchor line between my belt loops, tied
me in a midshipman's knot to the rail.
He lifted each of my hands, placing
my palms on the metal, curled
my fingers over and said, "Hang tight."

I heard it as "Hang five," thought of
"Hang Ten!" from *Gidget*, surfers each
riding high, each with ten toes perched
on the lip of their board–and now me
on the Chris-Craft's bow, steady,
with five real toes to hang.

Nodding, I inched my left toes over
the boat's bow, my plastic right foot
steady as a stork's, planted behind me
on the deck. And I've been
hanging five
ever since.

Yellow Time

The sly yellow gleam of sunlight
on spindly maple leaf wants
to pretend in Spring, to make believe
in the full tulip blooms beside the drive,
but nowhere does it tell you
how to make it stick,
how to stay whole,
even when parts are missing,
or when people go, and in this absence
pours some memory of youthful days
of trading toys, of not letting some
neighbor boy who knows better barter
for the Johnny West, when really
one loves Johnny, whose rubber hand
grips his toy coffee pot handle (he keeps
dropping the pistol), and the G.I. Joe
astronaut whose arms keep slipping
from their sockets, even as his pull tab
voice chants, with a hitch,

"Ten seconds to liftoff,
and count…ing."
The point is to maintain the self,
even if alone again, this time
beside a 1966 polka dot turn-table,
45rpm's with the yellow spindle adapter
that looks like three arms going
all the way around until it spins
and they blur into solid yellow,
the child singing alone, uneven
twirling in a circle, in time,
to time, of time.

The Flight Sonnets
for Danny

I.

A perfect match, we leave students
and whiteboards for wherever
they've stowed our old green table
with its dings and scratches and tilt.
Danny coaxes it toward balance
while I collect yesterday's game balls
into a cardboard box, as gingerly
as I'd pluck seashells or ripe berries.
When he's satisfied, we play, as both
campus and world dwindle.
There is only the thwack of paddles,
our banter to twenty-one, then again.
The white ball sails back and forth,
fueled by logic and by luck, in turn.

II.

A sign on the elevator, *Out of Use!*
At the stairs, I blanch to realize
he'll see me not as a contender,
not a poet to his engineer, but as one
who must take each step singly.
I long for falcon wings to unfurl
at my back, to lift me to the top.
But the only *flight* are the rising stairs.
While Danny follows me, one step
at a time, he begins a gentle monologue
about the rain, his classes, my dog,
I nod and take one step, another step.
Only later, I realize that sometimes
the other person becomes the falcon.

III.

At the landing, he glides past me
to hold the door, ever a gentleman,
and we go to either side of our table.
I search his gaze for the pity I fear,
but the grey eyes are steady, strong.
His first serve flies over the net,
too hard and fast for me to hit.
I grin and it happens twice more.

By the third time, I'm back to myself:
he has brought me back.
And he knows me after this, my sum,
and I know him, who he is in total.
Ping pong is not a wicked game,
but a game of love, played well.

Friday's Child, June 1963

A twilight Friday in June,
afternoon storm comes and goes,
leaves hot steam rising
from the Porky Pig Barbecue,
hickory smoke mixing with drizzle,
the big sun's parting wink
as he slides below
a shelf of charcoal clouds,
as a full Strawberry Moon
ascends opposite,
and a world of working folks
hits the weekend.

My mother waits
in the '56 Bel Air, watches
a pink Nash Cosmo nearly hit
a dark Packard, zip past and park,
people laughing in the warm buzz
under the neon; she feels baby
kick twice, two taps as though to ask
–*hello, hello out there?*
–*Too early*, she whispers,
fingers lightly on her belly,
as the Porky Pig sign
waves his glove
back and forth.

She watches the door:
it opens, closes, opens,
people laugh going in,
or hurry out with bags,
none of them her husband,
even as Porky Pig waves
hello, goodbye, hello,
and neon green flashes
"Friday Nite 2 for 1! YUM!"
and now a real contraction,
6:47, and again,
6:54, one more at
7:01, from baby due
in *August*, twelve weeks.

At 7:07, she calls to a couple
newly pulled in,
"My husband's in line,"
and describes his hair,
his name stitched on his shirt,
"Tell him *hurry*,"
This baby's not waiting
through the summer,
might not even wait
for husband or hospital.

Then he's there, panting,
the Bel Air's tires squeal:
behind them, Porky Pig
waves goodbye (or hello?).

The doctor at his cocktail party
swirls his martini olive
into an angry whirlpool.

Head Nurse relays from him:
"Go home, false alarm,"
and the couple sits unsure
until ten long minutes later
when the water breaks,
a puddle on linoleum,
and there's a rush—
nurses tell her to squeeze
her legs together.

I arrive half an hour later,
squalling, angry as the doctor,
himself newly sauntered in,
this being an evening
neither of us planned,
and with a belch he tells
the nurses to wrap me,
tells my mother
"Don't get too attached—
she'll be lucky to make it
to tomorrow," but he doesn't
mention the missing foot,
a sack, gives the nurses
a warning look
to keep quiet.

I am shuffled off
to the incubator room,
where other preemies
in their warm tents
clench, wriggle and hope
for morning, a field of hope
and possibilities, parents
staring through the glass,
nurses whispering.

I am lucky that night
and many more nights,
in my yellow-lighted
tent among tents.

I'm there and lucky
through the summer,
and fall, and by winter
it is clear: I aim to be
sticking around, foot or no foot,
something more than luck
at the core of this.

They walk in one cold night
in December, six months later,
to take me home, and I am
standing at the crib rail
of my tent:

I hold the bar with both hands,
grinning.

Fractions and Bones

by fractions that summer
we tested our fortitude
soaring over ditches
launching the unfit boat
past water moccasins,
revving engines our fathers
fashioned on their weekends,
we tested, flipping go carts
made from old push mowers,
racing yard sale mini bikes
through rising corn, even
urging tired ponies to speed,
and we, falling by fractions,
our bones tested, our child
laughter lingering in some
ancient corn crib.

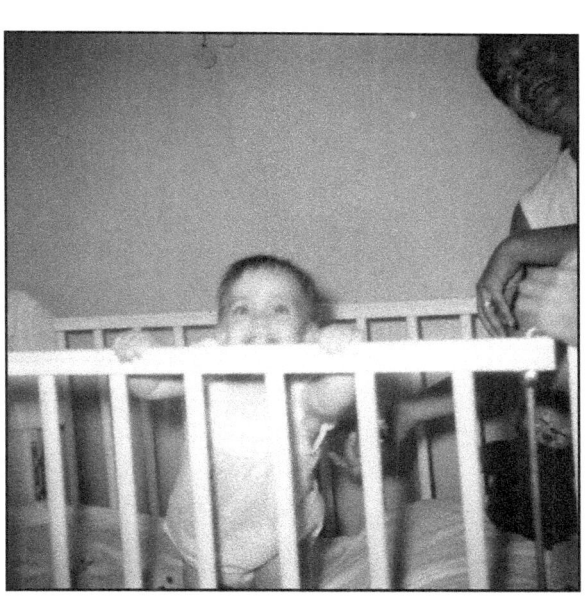

Jokes of Time

we watched that bumble
bore his holes, patient
buzzing under beams

too old to know, beams
from some Jester years
before we knew the joke

watched wood dust
sift down through barn air,
land silently, land soft

a cat descendent from
some long-ago cat also
watched the bumble

bore and drone one
hole, then another into
wood hardened by years
broken by insistence

Grandmother Minnie

She calls to me through cornfields
rough as her canvas scrub clothes,
calls me the "youngest daughter
of her youngest daughter" and places
her palm atop my head: I feel her
here, as I touch the new jars of pickles,
tomatoes, relish, and corn, lined
on a counter to get us through dark times;
I remember stories of her milking cows,
taking my mother, a girl, to the spring house,
where bubbling waters cooled the cream,
where, in the dimness, moments of escape
from the hot sun and the constant work
made them smile together.
I have lost them both except for my eyes,
they say, a certain rolling of the eyes
at a world gone mad, a world we must
walk away from sometimes, a lonely
trail of daughters.

Glow Worm Yellow

Tonight floating fast
by my window
the first firefly, and this,
barely Gemini's cusp.
I'm wondering: who will you find?
No one else is out this early, firefly.
You will live and die alone with your
pale blinking beacon, no one to answer
the call from the night cool grasses.

when I was young, I dreamed of fireflies
in 64 Crayola colors, drifting upward
from the lawn by the thousands:
Periwinkle was the most rare, but
Sea Green was my favorite.

Beside the swing-set,
Silver, Gold, and Copper glittered
like pirates' treasure as Brick Red
nearly collided with Burnt Sienna,
as Midnight Blue tagged Plum

Tonight the single blinker,
Firefly, Lightning Bug,
Glow Worm Yellow,
knows no colors but his own—
but what's this?
Now I see or think I see
another blink beneath
the Pine Green pine.
I close my eyes and wish it so.

Stowaways

There's an old stable just
over the hill, separating the house
from the fields, connected to a row
of smaller, also worn
wooden structures.

These saw varied use in their days,
a chicken coop with dusty windows,
a tack house, still two misshapen,
upright horseshoes nailed over
the door to hold in the luck.

On the far end is a corn crib,
taller than those and higher
up the incline, as if it takes
a proprietary view.
Its sides are slatted and wired,
so that the heavy yellow ears dry.
Bits of red cob and papery husks,
who knows how old, still dot
the rusted wire shaped like eyes
here and there.

This corn crib has seen
its share of stowaways—still
carries the ghosts of runaway slaves,
of clandestine lovers peeking
out the slats from the tall loft,
of a crying child whose bike
lay behind the crib in tall weeds—
who has run away from home,
but not very far from home,
determined never, ever
to return.

All four seasons loiter
here as well: the dense scents
of apple and pear blossoms,
aswirl with honeybees and
yellowjackets; the deep, soft dust
of the barn floor, baked
by hundred-degree summers;
a call-response of migrating geese
in their V, whirling leaves of red,
orange, and yellow; winter musk
of horses and hay hunkered near
a fort of straw built by the farmer
for his wide-eyed daughter child,
their breaths foggy in the chill,
mingling with the foggy snorts
of a forlorn, brown pony.

We were there as others
were there or will be there
or might be; the structures
themselves one day will fall.

We will fall. Our descendants
will fall, as our ancestors fell,
and that is neither sad nor precious.
It is not circular, nor especially cyclical.
It is the linear, unflagging
propulsion of time, through which
we are only temporary
stowaways.

I mention it not as a cynic,
nor in praise of humans
or nature or life.

I have no aim except
to stab a space, claim it,
to hold it still, to douse
the meteoric now.

Dreamtime Nocturne
Sestina

Over the hill, always at night, dreamtime
calls me to the slow bend in the creek, where
as a child I played a flute in noon woods
and mockingbirds paused their play to listen
while I offered naïve homage to their
swirling ancient notes, their collected songs.

Now, when I'm asleep, the nightingale's songs
fill the void, full moon rising low, dreamtime
shimmering on creek waters, songs in their
language-from-beyond, music asking where
spirit goes, where Music lives: I listen
to the chorus of questions in those woods.

The owl brings alto to these midnight woods,
a trio of bats pipe in with their songs—
dreamers the world over pause to listen,
drawn by song to the ethers of dreamtime,
pulled to this place, this bend in the creek where
sun and moon, real and unreal, have switched their

rhythms, accompanied by players, their
audience drawn in spirit to these woods,
wanderers all, harmony blending, where
every soul participates in these songs
running affrettando through the dreamtime,
voices rising on the night winds: listen!

So others, too, are drawn here to listen,
to sing, dreamers in this ensemble, their
nights entranced with a chorus of dreamtime
melodies that rise and fall through these woods,
as fog rising from the creek holds the songs,
the moon smiling broad above the oak, where

Music rises mysteriously, where
the seen and unseen beg us to listen,
to join the raucous chorus with our songs,
each spirit with accompaniment, their
voices echoing through silver moon woods
winding round a burbling creek in dreamtime,

a place where you, too, will be called to their
show, to listen to the sound of the woods:
bring songs, join the orchestra of dreamtime.

Because It's Nighttime Again
Rocky Point State Park, Rhode Island, 1974

It was after Electric Boy,
though his legend remained:
his armless high dives into
the salt water pool, stories
passed between us in the back seat
on the way to Rocky Point, and he
remains there still, I believe, perched
on the highest dive, armless as a fish,
all eyes upon him, his flawless descent,
ghost diver, maimed from his climb
over the fence, not to bypass the price,
but to show he *could*, his armless
yearly return each summer
a testament to all childhood valor.
His ghost from the high dive salutes
Babe Ruth, of a different decade,
pitching for the Providence Grays,
hits a home run into Narragansett Bay.
With them both, an open trolley still runs

from Providence for "Summer Fun
in the Rhode Island Sun," as hurricanes
strike and strike again, and level
Shore Dinner Hall, clamsbake heaven,
even as the light-up Bingo Board
buzzes and someone screeches inside
the Castle of Terror; all of these at once
share the same nonlinear space,
impulses of memory: a man clips
onto my wrist a coral-colored string
that shows I've paid for All Day & All Night,
top of the log flume full moon smiling,
as one-two-three Hugo Zacchini
the human projectile soars across
the nighttime Midway, now fairy tale,
a Rocky Point collective unconscious.

Somewhere in Florida

We sit sweating at a snake show,
Mr. Snake-handler wants volunteers,
Mom sick with fear, "phobia" too weak a word,
Dad urging me to raise my hand, "Go on, go on!"

I do, am ushered up, lifted onstage:
over my neck, they drape a snake
so long that both ends touch the floor,
tickling wet on my neck, and I laugh.
"Hold still, little guy," I whisper.

Merging

A-Side
"Come to the Light!"

We two tool around the pool,
cousin Tanya and me, subdued
because the adults have argued,
as Aunt Eva reads, other motel kids
splash in, and I hide by the steps,
holding myself under, curling arms
and legs around the metal railing.
I am stuck underwater, knotted
by my own entwined limbs,
unable to move, gulping water,
lungs burning: it goes dark.

I am pulled out, Aunt Eva's voice,
"Breathe, baby, breathe…!"
Water burbles out of me,
air-in means I'm alive again,
the sun through palm fronds.

How the strangers look on:
the woman and a footless girl,
older child clutches a leg brace.

–Is she okay? What's wrong with her?
–She doesn't 'look' okay.

Even at three, I know I'd have died;
for days, I refuse to leave our room.
I don't know how I get from there
to the B-Side.

B-Side
"I Will Catch You"

He sets me atop the pool slide,
Daddy, my hero, so high I see
the motel roof, coconuts, but below,
a wide, blue plane of water,
beyond, my mother and Aunt Eva,
displeased with him, afraid for me,
beside the metal railing.

He says, "Hold your nose," and then,
"Wait for me and I will catch you."

I nod, slide fast, plunge deep
into water, slow sinking as bubbles
brush up past me, my cheeks puffed,
I wait, am waiting, sinking,
waiting, until he scoops me out,
us both laughing hard
in the sweet, hot sun.

Do it again.

Homing Instincts

Where I am now
Two sets of geese in "V"'s
Coast in for a landing on the pond
Beside the mountain, flapping and happy
For the rest.

Where I come from
Ten thousand of these fellows will gather
On my father's fields, a nation
Of wanderers, a hundred tribes
On their way, on their way soon.

Now, a single goose approaches, stops,
Stands on one leg, cocking his head.
He's stopped here, where I am now
On his way to where I'm from:
In his eye I read the message.

Weekends at the Longs'

A-Side

Only child, I'm used to silences, long days,
coloring books of my own scribbles,
hide and seek where no one seeks.

So, on those weekends we went
to St. Leonard's, I'd feel scooped up
by the happy pack of "Long Girls,"
five daughters, my semi-cousins,
freckles and shrieks, tugging me
from the car, Aunt Barbara, Uncle Eddie
asking how-are-you, my voice
ziffed away in a scale of girl buzz.

Also-Sandy and Annie-E buoy me
into the kitchen, as blonde little Penny
follows, then Pam and Lynn, teenage
Pageant Queens who wear make-up
and date boys, who chat with my parents,
and haul in our suitcases.

It is late morning and the kitchen
blooms with bacon frying, dark coffee
bubbling in the percolator's glass eye
beside a hissing skillet as Aunt Barb
cracks an egg or three, as plates appear,
a dozen, and flatware, a gallon of o.j.,
napkins with roses on them, Uncle Eddie's
baritone as he says I'm getting taller,
as he tells Dad it's an easy fix,
to change those hard leg-brace straps
cutting into my leg, for the supple
Italian leather he got as reins for his
dapple-grey mare— he winks at me,
"We'll up your horse power!"
His chuckle runs warm currents,
Aunt Barbara says "Give that girl toast,"
and toast appears on my plate.

Later, I waver when told it's time
to take off my leg, but Uncle Eddie
kneels and places his huge hand atop
my head—Fire Chief, Smokey the Bear
in the St. Leonard's parade, he promises,
"Lickety-split, you'll be raring to go,"
a solid ken amid many faces, voices,
scents, colors, and so I slip it off,
as Also-Sandy and Annie-E turn me,
put Lite-Brite on my lap, a joy of neon
colors I have never known, a boat,
a sun, a rearin' to go horse of lights.

B-Side

After the leg is fixed, softer straps,
a Band-aid on the blisters, the girls
take me upstairs to play "The Dating Game,"
a spinner moves your pieces, the suitors

appear at random when you open the door,
and I struggle to know why some of them
are funny and bad to find at your door,
but I can see in the smiling eyes of the girls
some knowing I will come to know
on the Order of such things,
except that years later I will dream
myself in a gender opposite game,
some boy opening the game door
and me there, me there, and all
of the boys hooting at
such a bad outcome for him,
and me there, trapped behind
the door and unable to speak
or move.

Dream Landing

I remember being small,
some party my parents toted
me to, blue shadows,
streetlight shining on cars
in the drive, hot laughter
as the door opened and all
the adults with greetings,
me shuffled forward, met,
and handed off to a child
running the tribe of offspring
who had their own games,
didn't notice me and
so I edged my way back
toward the front door,
and as they raced away upstairs
I slid through a side door,
a landing with steps down
to an empty, finished room
with a washer/dryer and a rug.

Weary, I settled there at the top,
my legs on the steps, the clink
of bottles, laughter behind me
in the room of adults, no one
knowing I was there, or where
I might be, no matter,
I had begged to come, to not be
left with a sitter again, or Nana
who liked to pinch my cheeks
hard, very hard, harder than
was nice to do to a child
too worn to protest, Nana who
liked for me to show my fake leg
to her friends, when they visited,
to show them I was not ashamed,
not at all ashamed, that I was fine.

I dream this place, the landing,
me removed from them all,
no one wondering where
I'd gotten off to and perhaps
I slept in the purple shadows
looking down on the washer,
my head pressed to the wall.

Get Your Own

You know, it's the volts that'll get you,
not the amps, he said.
Lightning struck Nana three times,
they said: the third time
blew her shoes of her feet.

At fourteen, I cursed to upset
my mother, at the stove,
where she fussed with me—
so I declared, "God is not real."
I glared out the window,
across a spring green rye-field,
aqua sky with sheep-clouds,
and I sent my challenge upward:
If You are there– prove it.

From that blue sky, a bright
white bolt zagged down,
electric, striking the field.
It rattled our windows.

"That wasn't thunder?" Mom asked.
I couldn't answer; forty years later,
still have no answer, except this:
on a blue-sky day, from nowhere,
came a retort, as if to say both
Watch yourself – and
– I hear you.

You have to get your own volts,
I think.

Who Cooks for You?
for Danny

We meet as though just passing time,
like grackles on the wire, chirping
about the day's deeds, until two robins
in the grass beneath the cedar tease,
Could we? Could we?
and cardinals start flirting
Pretty, pretty, pretty
from the dogwood.

I'm not sure we've known
each other long enough for this,
but the black and white warbler hints
Let's see, let's see, let's see.

(Could we sweep down from the wire,
Pretty pretty, and then find ourselves
Beneath a tree, let's see,
Let's see?)

Cherry blossom petals
freckle the sidewalk as twilight
swallows slice the gloaming,
winking and chirping seductively,
Sure we can, we can,
while gentle mist lifts
toward the street lamps.

Maybe the sparrow's right,
Yes, yes, yes, oh my gosh, yes!
The yellow warbler adds

Be easy, easy, be easy,
here in the soft chill of
New Spring, and the barred owl asks
Who cooks for you, who cooks for you?
Safely on her nest, the chickadee speaks:
Me... Me.

Red Bike, Red Keds

Along the street to Mayo Beach,
beside each front step or garage,
tossed in next to trash cans under
dusty windows full of paint cans,
lay bikes and trikes of all shapes,
and parts of those, wheels, seats,
baskets, though never
a helmet (ever).

We carved dust trails
beside the street in packs
of two or six or ten, racing hard
or not, careful not to stray close
to the fence in which mellow cows
chewed, but also where (Moms said)
a raging half-crazed bull, with horns
like devil-spears, waited for us.

At five, I was hindered by
training wheels on a little red bike,
hindered by parents who warned me
to go slow, who worried my fake leg
would dump me into the street or
into a field with a half-crazed bull
as I tried to keep up with the others.

But Alfie, who was eight, pointed:
"Them trainin' wheels hobble you."
The phrase haunted me, "hobble,
to walk with a limp," or "hobble,
a torture involving to
crush the ankle bones,"
or "to hobble a horse by
fastening his legs together
so that he doesn't stray."

They had hobbled me,
and all I wanted was to be cut
loose from the little wheels,
to be free to stand in the seat,
pedaling faster than anyone,
the small red bike racing ahead.

I begged my father that night
after supper, "Take them off."
He lectured, explained, teased,
declined, and next night got mad,
lost his temper, next went silent—
four days into my siege, relented.

I sat in the gravel as he turned
the wrench, as he grumbled,
"You'll *fall, hurt* yourself, come
crying to me, and I'll put the damn
things back on for good."

I nodded, picturing it, vowing
to myself I'd be gored by a devil-bull
or die on the asphalt before ever
come crying back: can you
imagine such a five-year-old?

And when he was done,
I looked at the training wheels
flat in the grass and I got on
my red bike, felt him steadying
the seat with his hand, guiding me
as I started to pedal and shift
for balance, heard his quick breath,
knew he feared for me, but then
I launched myself forward and stood
and pedaled harder than ever
and left his steadying hand
and never fell
and never looked back.

Green Bike

Some days, when walking
seems impossible,
I dream of a green bike,
sour apple green or maybe
mint with small, cream tires,
a collapsible rack for books,
and a small, tooting horn
for when I'm coasting toward
a crosswalk and see a friend,
or riding down the Tweetsie
and want to hear the echo
in the underpass, in fact,
a bike I can fold in half,
slipping it into the back
of the hatch or sliding
it into a suitcase 'cause
I might take it to Key West,
my green, folding bike,
and bike down Whitehead to

Hemingway's House
or the Southernmost Point,
me and the green bike
of my dreams being
inseparable like that.

What We No Longer Know

He no longer knows where
the thermostat is nor where it used to be,
though when I say "hallway," he hesitates,
and then I ask, like I always ask:
—*Where are you?*

Today he knows he's in the kitchen,
though one day soon, he won't know
what the *kitchen* is, though he might
be able to tell me, then, "There's a stove,"
just as he told me last week,
"My bed is upstairs."

We are having one of seven
phone conversations he won't remember,
though he knows I call, "now and then,"
he told Aunt Mary Lou, and God knows
what she thinks or thought of me or how
the cousins process this, probably not
as harshly as I imagine,
probably with deep compassion.

He wants to know—*Where are you?*
I'm five hundred miles from him,
in a small brick house with two dogs,
one of them once my mother's, my mother
who begged me to bring the Jack Russell
five hundred miles so he'd be safe,
"Spotz," who pisses on the lower shelf
of my bookcase three times a day,
and I tell myself I'm lucky
he's not any taller, as I tell myself
I'm lucky the libation my father sneaks
to town to get is only Ensure.

It makes him sick, as he chugs down
five or six bottles at a time, telling me,
if he's found out, "It's only chocolate milk,"
an argument we repeat weekly, since
Ensure makes him forget to heat pizza
in the Kmart microwave I got him
with the twist-dial because he no longer
understood the punch-in number one,
my mother's before she left us here
in this muddle, and died.

It is Ensure he sneaks off to buy,
not vodka, and he might not know
the thermostat is in the hallway,
but he still knows what one does,
just as he knows Mom is not coming back,
neither of us asking her, though both of us
wondering in our ways,
Where are you?

Wind Tokens

I spoke to the wind today
remembered mother hushing me,
standing behind me at some long ago
window, whispering, *Never, never*
speak to the wind, my darling.
I asked why, then, my ever-question,
but she only shook her head, glanced
beyond me to the leaves stirred to wild
circles, to the flapping wild white arms,
father's shirts on the line come alive,
as above us some attic shutter slapped
the side of the old house for emphasis.

Pop Tops

Pop tops, the old ones,
pull tab connected to the curly,
shiny on a sand-glazed blacktop.

Jim Jr., a cousin, collected them,
his palm out whenever the folks
gathered to drink beer in striped
lawn chairs at twilight, citronella
floating up from netted candles,
flames attracting cautious moths.
.
He had freckles, I remember,
made a pop top chain mail blanket,
hung it across his bedroom wall—
that's a lot of Pabst—joined the
Merchant Marines and maybe
killed himself, I heard, though I'd
lost track of that branch by then.

Sideshow, Davidsonville Elementary

A-Side

Tuesday, September 2nd, 1969,
written high on the board beneath
the ABC's, me and the others—
shell shocked as the bell trills
Recess!, Recess!, and we rise,
ragged group of first graders,
into a sunny hall, until from
nowhere The Upper Graders,
as a herd of moose crashing
into us, around, over, past us,
our exploding pencil boxes of
penguin-shaped erasers,
jumbo pencils, peace-sign stamps
rattling down as double-doors
slam shut on the outside;
we remain alone in the wake
of our sundry goods, myself teary

at sight of the alligator stapler,
his upper jaw filled with staples
detached from his lower.

Tough, tiny Amy Hardesty helps me,
says, "So, kid, it's true about your leg?"

I nod and she says, "Show me."

I lift my pants, show how the stump
sans foot slides in/out of the fake leg.
I slide it halfway, twirl it in a circle.

She grins and leads me out,
to the back side of the school,
a place unwatched by teachers,
and says "Wait here."

Come one, Come all,
I imagine her calling across
the playground, like a kid barker
announcing a circus freak show.

She returns with six Upper Graders,
claims, "This kid twirls her foot
in a whole circle, without moving
the rest of her: *a quarter to see it.*"

The Upper Graders smirk, but Amy
says, "No lie, no psyche, one quarter,"
and they say they'll knock her stupid
if it's some trick.

"No trick," she says, waiting to see
them show their quarters; two leave,
but six more arrive, ten in all.

When she nods at me, I slide my leg
up enough to touch fake toes-in-shoe
to the dirt and spin the leg full-circle,
around and around, an illusion of
of a foot able to spin freely about,
as though my knee has no joint.
.

They gasp, impressed, satisfied,
and hand over their quarters, then
head off across the playground to
broadcast my inhuman feat.

Amy separates our take in half,
five quarters for me, five for her,
"Get yourself a new alligator stapler,"
she says, and adds, "We'll do it again,
and next time charge more."

And we do.

B-Side

During recess, we have our friends,
our echelon, generally safe except
for war-time in which factions
go against each other and favors
are called in for allies, deeper bonds
and stricter conduct rules than adults
fathom "in kids"—adult amnesia.

I am happy in my groups, choose
between them, given my mood,
except when the going-in-bell rings,
for as we head 'back to building,'
pulling ourselves into class lines,
as our teachers start out for us,
there comes each day a blurry moment,
separate from our recess platoons,
not quite within teachers' range—
when I am culled from the rest
by this pair of boys, strangers to me,
for special bullying.

They hold lower rank than I do,
but take the unclaimed slice of day
to encircle me, pushing, the smaller
one in charge, slapping me, calling
me "fatso," the taller one less verbal,
but pushing hard as I spin and try
to block them and keep my balance.

And I know, and they know,
my daily disadvantage here will
soon begin to "mark me," despite
my higher rank, prompting others
to join in the attack– how it worked
and still works among mammals
young and old.

They leave off as teachers
draw closer, but my time
is running out on this.

Then one day, I snag the shirt
of the shorter, the leader, clutch it,
and hurl him onto his back in the dirt:
I straddle him, my knees pinning
his arms to his sides, while the larger
boy gapes, backs off, others
encircling now, cheering for blood–
the whole of their daily torment
boils in me.

"Say you're sorry," I demand,
and he does, tears in his eyes,
the crowd jeers him, Amy Hardesty's
voice clear: *Break his nose! Break it!*

Instead, I slap his face hard
enough to leave a bright stripe,
and I yell, "Say it again! Louder!"

He does, and I hit him harder, repeating
myself, and again he cries "I'm sorry,"
and again I hit him, and he sobs—
and the crowd around us *applauds*.

Then, stillness except his ragged breath,
and a lady teacher I don't know
stands above us, her eyes holding
all the knowledge of every recess
ever held, somehow, and she shrugs,
says, "He's probably had enough…"

It is not a demand: if I want to,
this lady teacher is giving permission
to hit him again—I know it, he knows it,
and the crowd of my peers know it.

I see him then, his burbling tears,
the blotchy slap-prints on his cheeks,
his hair smeared into the dirt, and so
I nod, and the lady teacher—
this part matters—helps me up,
but leaves him there.

Learn to Fall

We sold the boat to buy
the farm, my father's dream,
but not my mother's, whose
folks had been sharecroppers,
who'd married a man who
wanted a boat, and not,
she liked to point out,
a farmer.

Not that farming meant
he quit his full-time job,
no, farming would be
nights, weekends, mornings,
everything in between, enough
tomato plants and fence painting
to take up all of our time,
unlike a boat.

Even at six years old,
I was not a fan of farming,
appeasement coming in the form
of an irascible Chincoteague pony
named Brownie, for which
all the girls at school envied me:
a pony I longed to trade
for a boat.

I did not ask for the pony,
but each day I trudged
to the stable, where he glared
from under a blonde forelock
as I bridled and saddled him,
lofted myself onto his back:
"Giddyup," I'd urge—he'd fart
in response.

I'd cluck and click, lightly
kick his sides, but Brownie
would wait until I let down
my guard before rearing up
and then bolting from the barn
like some rodeo sideshow,
me clinging to the reins,
trying to keep balance.

Those were "riding lessons"
in the ancient 1970's–
they were free, and if
you didn't die, you learned
to ride; more than that,
you learned how to fall,
how to let go of success
while sailing through the air.

I sailed through the air a lot:
Brownie broached rose hedges,
and when next day I got back on,
he skirted the barbed wire fence,
(luckily along my right side),
big gashes on my plastic leg;
I bailed off when he swung
about to try the other side.

No, really, there are lessons
to learn from bailing off, even
from landing hard enough to
knock the wind out of you,
to lie there gasping for air
and hoping you do not die,
and that no one sees you,
while the pony smirks.

He'd crush me into the fence,
and once, on a cold March day,
he ran right down the steep hill
into the pond, deep enough for
the icy water to cover his legs,
then mine, and then he stopped,
waited, until finally I bailed off
and swam back to shore.

At night, the grownups would
laugh as my mother told how
each day she'd watch me ride
out of the barn, and each day
Brownie came back riderless,
how she'd hold her breath
until I came trudging back
alone, wet or torn or muddy.

Learn to ride, my darlings,
but above all, learn to fall.

Ode to Mrs. Hutchinson

Like an ox, she stared me down,
a slow blink, me there trapped
at a desk, eight years old.
I want that box of cowboy stamps
and ink to make a page of wild west stories:
cactus will dot the title line, a cowboy
riding the margin, chasing two calves toward
the middle loose-leaf binder hole.

Or else, I want out:
I'm eight-year-old eager for the May sun,
for the internal-organ colored kickball
pitched hard and wafting down a dusty lane—
best kicker in the 3rd grade,
I'm a legend.

Just the week before
Mrs. Hutchinson had me there,
I kicked so hard my fake leg flew
over the pitcher's head to second base
while the ball flew into far left,
a home run, a real beauty,
but I stood one-legged, stork-like, stunned,
as Jerry Blickstein yelled "Ghost runner!"
and red-haired Carrie sprinted by.
After the point, after she crossed home,
they brought my leg,
grinning.

And still this woman stared down
her glasses at me until I faced the paper
once again, one hundred cursive C's lacking
their leading stroke (again).

Someone grabbed my box of stamps.

The bell trilled and I put the pencil to a 'C'
even as my kickball team
hurried into the bright hotness.

I glanced up.
"Go," she said,
without a smile.

Yard Circles

hot Chesapeake night, I wonder
why they were outside, the adults,
in a circle, like a powwow, around a fire,
the smoke, someone said to keep off the
mosquitoes, though it didn't, or
we were too far away, dodging
around the Russian olive tree
with its monolith branches twisting
monster shadows by the fire,
the cherry where earlier that year
the boys had climbed and picked
and eaten, not knowing there were worms,
ha ha, and now us running past and around
the circle of parents drinking hard, vodka,
Jim Beam, their whispers and sharp laughs
mingling with the crackle of fire.

Later, they switched to beer and we,
sweaty from play had settled against
the metal side of the above-ground pool,
the bunch of us until someone, not me, said:
they're so drunk they won't notice
if we fill their beer bottles with pool water.

Without deciding to, fully, we made a plan,
one belly crawling over the tufted lawn,
elbows and knees, skinny arm reaching

over the space between their flipflops, loafers,
workboots, to grasp a bottle, pass it back,
kid to kid, dumping it beside the pool and
refilling with chlorine tinged liquid, then back,

kid to kid, and placed beside a tapping foot.
They drank without knowing and we huddled
in our own circle in the grass behind them
howling with glee, repeating it
time and again.

Hallowafternoon to E'en

Unseasonably balmy, so we kids ride
in the back of the green wagon
pulled behind the corn-picker
pulled behind the old red
Massey-Ferguson.

The open blue sky flutters
with papery husks, hot corn
smell like spoon-bread frying
as heavy ears, stripped from stalks
ride up the chain and shoot down at us,
banging onto the wagon floor, popping
sun yellow kernels from pocked ears.
They rise around as we count the rows,
and gauge how many to go
how many rows now,
eager for E'en.

Tonight we'll ride
in the bed of the '69 Ford pickup
as the folks drive us to 'burbs
out by Central Avenue,
homes of the rich kids, some of them
 our friends.

Little Roy is a bloodied mummy,
borrowing Big Roy's crutches,
torn white sheet and a lot of ketchup.

Debbie is older, but comes anyway
in a gypsy scarf, her story about
a sick (non-existent) kid sister,
a bag we'll hand our drivers,
who do not complain,
who ride three abreast on the bench seat
drinking beer and creeping along the road
with an eye on us as they share Almond Joy,
Reese's, and orange and black wrapped taffy.

David is Billy the Kid in crumpled,
cowboy hat and a yellow scarf,
while I'm a vampire in a black silk shirt
Mom bought me at the Sears store
and fangs that glow in the dark,
corn chaff still in my hair.

Sanctus Peninsula

Station wagon leather seats heated
by a Fall River sun, old wagon
winter parked beneath a mulberry,
abandoned factory smokestacks sky,
but we'd ride, ride on as soon in June

as schools set us free, drawn to the fist,
as I saw it then and see it now,
curled arm showing muscle to the world,
as we'd ride up 6A, past Brewster,
pit stop at Franny's for the fried clams,

on again, Eastham, Wellfleet, Truro,
bitter winters receding, windows
open to salt marsh infusion, gulls
on one side, herons on the other,
I am both inside the car and out.

I am young again each June, back seat
waiting for the old wagon to stop,
release us into sea air and dunes
that beg to be topped and trundled,
a pull instinctual to the sea.

And still the Cape summons me from points
landlocked, places mundane with workdays,
as sanctus bells beckon the faithful
to lift their minds above the daily,
just as now I go to Provincetown.

Ahab's Day
For Linda Ferreira, Rehoboth, Massachusetts 1974

You, they said
I was ten, a
one-legged girl
new to town.

What.
You come here,
they said
the asphalt hot,
sticky smells of tar
and dog poop
glints of green and yellow
from the stained glass
church windows,
all empty now on
a Thursday in
May.

Is it wood?
They were bigger
than me,
taller with big teeth
snarling as they
looked at the
panted leg.

Yeah.
Though it was plastic,
no matter, nothing
to them.

Call her Ahab,
one said, but
so what, so what,
I was waiting as usual
for a ride, and they were
nothing to me.
Held out the hockey stick,
Do you play.
No.

Stand here.
She pointed between two
moved trash cans
that smelled of car oil
and old McDonalds bags.

They held the stick
flat, like a sword for me,
chins tucked in,
asking with their eyes,
pointing.

I took it, the wood to me
like a tobacco stick from
back home, where life
made more sense
than here,
the pale cream colored
blade scratched, etched
from many church lot
afternoons.

The tallest girl grinned:
Lead with the peg-leg,
keep your good one back,
push with the stick–
hit 'em hard on the shins:
never back down,
and, whatever you do,
don't let the ball past
this line.

Ahab stuck,
as a name: I played hard,
heard the other team's sticks
slap against the plastic, felt
the jarring, but no pain,
bared my teeth at them,
sent the red ball a dozen yards
the other way,
then cracked their shins
for good measure.

Two Packs of Kools
for Vernon, Eileen, and Jerry

The summer I'm sixteen, Vern and Eileen
Rothschild give me a job at their prosthetics shop,
the cool glass front office, the dusty back room
full of fake legs, arms, iron braces, boxes and bags,
a neatly jumbled conglomerate of work and care.

I fetch and tidy, and I watch, and they teach me.
Jerry teases, "We'll let you make your own leg,
if yours breaks," and Vernon adds, "The catch is,
you have to make it without any help,"
meaning 'on one leg.'

We laugh together, then, at ourselves, Vernon,
too, with a fake leg (one he made himself).

The heat in the D.C. suburb steams the tar,
and Jerry tells me to go to 7-Eleven, gives me
$5 for two packs of Kools and a Slurpee for me.
"Take your time, come back through the front,
hang out in the office 'til we give an all clear,"
though usually I cross the back lot to 7-Eleven.
It means someone's coming in with a loss too real
for strangers to see, like the kid in the work room
who pushes a broom and picks up the Kools.

When I come in the front, Eileen gives me lunch
orders for Friendly's, they always buy my lunch,
too, and by the time I return with cartons,
the patient has come and gone.

Lunch is quiet that day, a kind of respect
for the loss that still hangs in the air,
a loss that can't be fixed with a fiberglass leg,
though it sure as hell beats not having one.

I busy myself tidying each table and bench,
as Vernon has taught me, organizing tools,
putting away equipment, rolls of casting plaster,
leather, nails, and empty Kool packages, using the
stiff brush then to wipe away debris, so that
each day the work room starts fresh, so that
each day begins new.

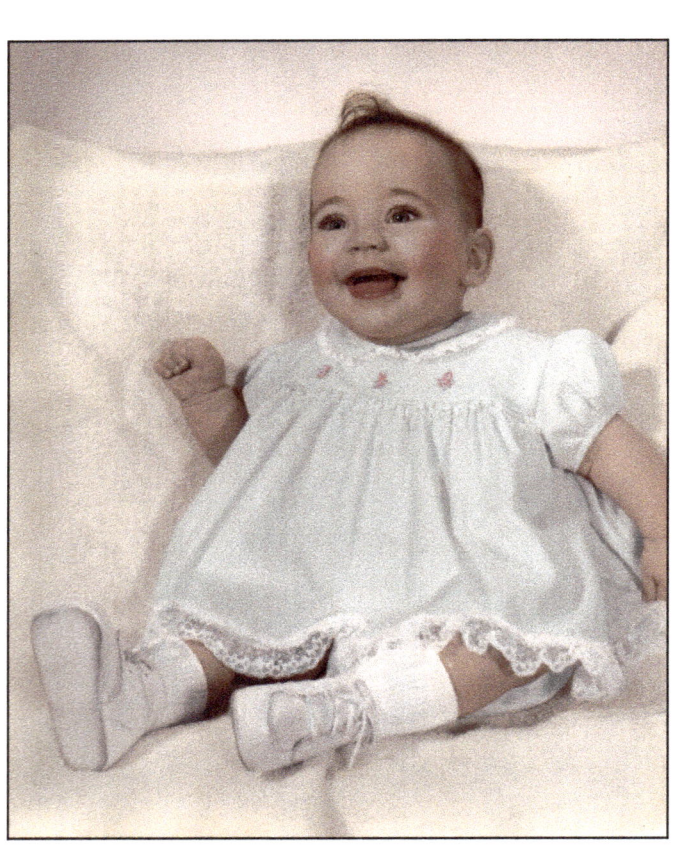

Dixon Sale on Wednesdays

I. The First

"I like it," I said, as the tired buyers
crowded our auctioneer's cart,
bidding and buying, nearer, dusty,
thirsty, thinking of home.

Mom and I had trod all day
the seven-acre field, up and down rows,
Who will give me ten? so now she smiled
bemused at the wrecked china closet
tipping leftward in the grasses,
its window busted, its once oak sides
flaking black, a marriage atop a
mahogany drawer without pulls.

All day I'd liked things, but,
too timid, had not bid. "Get ready," she said
as the cart rolled up, to this last piece
of the day, as Johnny our auctioneer grinned,
"Who will start at *ten*?"
No one stirred, "So who will do *seven*?"
People coughed and looked away, sheepish,
"Five? Just *five* for this—this—um—" laughter,
and then, "Will *anyone* give us a *buck* for this?"
"I will!" I yelled and "Sold!" he said, and Mom
grinned and hugged me close. And so
Reindeer Valley Antiques was born.

II. Spotz

All day at Dixon's and the truck full,
I stood in the long line inside to pay,
leaning on the counter, shoulder to shoulder
with big sweaty folks, dealers from Brooklyn,
Georgia, Texas, and also dainty local types,
me alone, having made a good haul,
a scratched library table for fifteen, a seat-less tiger
stripe oak rocker, two boxes of lamps and lamp
parts, a rug, a tobacco stand. I would profit.

I heard laughter and a tick-clicking of claws:
a Jack Russell terrier walked the high counter,
picking his way over and around arms, hands,
checkbooks, as though on a mission.
He got to me, stopped, curled himself
into the crook of my left arm, settling atop
my checkbook as everyone chuckled.
An orphan, someone said, *wandering alone*,
Until now. He rode in the front seat, wagging.
Mom asked, "Did you bring me something good?"
"I did," I said, and grinned. "Come see."

III. The Ladies

We wandered that day on 'the good side'
after all was done, the dealers departed,
we being 'vultures,' hunting for discards.
Mom saw them first, the ladies in their yellow
dresses, statuesque, plaster lamps, 1940's,
"But one," she said, "Is missing her head."

We took the other, though sad to split the pair,
and wandered on for other treasures.
Twenty yards north, beside a wicker mess,
Mom called, "It's here—her head is here!"
She held up the baseball-sized lady's head,
its smile equally shy despite decapitation,
despite being kicked along in the dust
so far from her sister, not to mention her body.
Mom put the head in her purse as we
made our way back and set head on neck
a perfect fit, a triumphant reunion.

For a dozen years or more those girls have sat
on either side of whatever sofa I have in whatever
living room of whatever state I'm in now.

Hand Over Hand

Pure ice cold steel rungs up
the side of the hay wagon on
this March day and I'm never
going to get up the side this time,
can feel as I kick with the right leg,
no traction with this prosthesis, can't find
this next rung, as the real leg that thinks
it has a foot like the other leg has, tries to catch
each rung like the left foot does, but
misses each time the connection so I
must pull with my hands and arms,
must pull as the left foot compensates.
It is only a hay wagon and nothing more,
nothing my life depends upon—
there's no reason at my age,
nearly forty then, to try and make
this climb again, to be the one atop
the bales when they come out after
breakfast to start unloading.

I could, I know, drop back, as only
the single steer named "Jimbo" has seen
me climb halfway up, has offered his
grunting support, perhaps hoping
I'll toss him a bale if I ever get up there.
I could drop back, lower myself
each rung down and land back where
I started and no one would know the better.
For a moment, I hang, undecided,
gripping the cold, knowing I must find
the rung to the right with a plastic right foot
or risk falling halfway up.
And then I do it anyway.
I close my eyes and climb
all the way to the top without
letting myself think of falling:
and I throw Jimbo his bale.

Median
to my parents

I've tried to leave you behind,
at the Rest-Stop in my dreams,
the one in the highway median,
18-Wheelers, station wagons,
and Harleys rushing by on either side,
and in the middle, in my dream,
so many cars, but also glass-blowers,
funnel cakes, warring tribes, actual tribes
or Mardi Gras "tribes," and my dog with me,
crazy Gidget loosely leashed,
disappearing and reappearing
and I keep asking all the folks,
"how do I get back on my road?"

They stop their glass blowing,
their dough frying, to tell us and,
grateful, I leave but realize
I've lost the car and cannot even
remember what color it is,
let alone make and model,
and I scan those many cars,
Gidget eager: was it maroon?

I find one that looks like ours,
but as we approach I find I am
turned around again and no longer know
which side of the highway
I should be driving toward.

so we head back to the middle,
around the tribes,
now a parade, now a wedding party
and limo, now a baseball team
all with snow cones in red and blue,
and we head back to ask
someone else, which way?

Finally I am yelling, "Which way
to Johnson City?"

Because I know I can't go back,
won't go back, whatever is back there,
the other way – and you are back there –

I don't want it. I want forward.
Any car, dog at my side,
forward into my life,
with or without blown glass or
funnel cakes or baseball games
or parades.

Bench

It's just a bench, my hand
comes down flat upon, a bench
made from a walnut tree that stood
wide over the sky in front of what was
a milk barn before we bought the farm
thirty years ago and turned it into what was
a calving shed, until that tree—

that looked "like Africa" from my room
at sunset (a tree that once popped me
on the head with a walnut as I passed by,
which sounds funny but wasn't),

a tree wherein a great horned owl
would sit on winter nights and low hoot three times,
his deeply wooden call echoing in the topless silo
beside it –

a tree that grew waterlogged one spring
and

fell backwards over the calving shed,
destroying the center of that barn,
the huge root ball, twelve feet across
pointing toward the house in defeat,
a tree's life well lived…

I was gone by then, they sent me photos,
and Dad had the tree lumbered into
dark boards to make a wide, fine bench
for me to bring back to Tennessee.

Nature of Dementia

In some ways it's no different from ever,
his hating his life as he leans stiff-backed
on a tan bedspread, teeth clenched,
growling like some wild dog and I fear
it'll disturb snoring Mel, his roommate in this
 A-D unit, the dementia ward, which
other than lock-down alarms and crazy folk,
seems like any nursing home—

no different from his hating a July drought
one year after two months of Spring floods
tricked corn seeds into sprouting shallow roots
unable to reach deeply enough for water,
waist-high plants roasting into
tan husks in the field.

The Stevens boys, our neighbors,
would say you can't tell about weather,
no predicting her, old school farmers
who didn't irrigate, at peace with Fate.

How they marveled at my Dad's angst,
his need to control his world, acting like
the business manager he'd been all his life,
as if to order the clouds, threaten the sun,
as now he seeks order in a mind that tricks
him sideways, though the angst stems
from the same ceaseless desire for better,
better, better, in all things, though nature
simply and honestly, is only itself.

Returning

I moved here, transplant of
Northern climes, to the former home
of a plant aficionado, one like my mother
with an intuition for flora: blooms appear
mysteriously about the yard.
Each set goes, replaced in
clockwork profusion— crocuses,
tulips, daffodils, and then roses,
iris, and three kinds of lily.

In December, when Mom came
to live with me, I promised her
the winter would end, and then
she'd see the boldest, brightest blooms
ever seen, red and yellow tulips
around the statue of St. Michael
just outside our front window.
I'll cut a few and bring them in, I said,
if you can't go out to see. *I will.*

In January, at the hospital, her sill
overflowed with gift flowers
as outside the snow swirled above roads
against a mountain scrim
still new to her.

We held each other's hand and watched
the snow fall and fall and
we tried to believe in the Spring.

By February, I asked hospice
to bring her home to me,
as red and yellow tulips
hovered in our imaginary future,
a warmth to come, full of color,
full of nectar, a time ahead.
It was a dream we inhaled.
She died as I held her,
four days later.
Our tulip time was
nowhere near.

Back North we went.
Her sky-blue casket
on a metal bier, draped
with greenhouse flowers,
taken to a small plot, a marble vault
carved with Tolkien's words,
 "Moonlight drowns out
all but the brightest stars,"
the vault beneath an aged cherry tree,
within whose blooms the birds will nest,
the best I could do and so little, it seems.

I sit at the window and see
red and yellow tulips in bloom,
in April grandeur, for us.
Planted by some other owner,
they yearly return to say
simply that they will return.
They will.

And I'm still hanging on,
still hanging five.

About the Author

Sandy Hiortdahl received the Sophie Kerr Prize, The Ghost Mountain Award, and several distinctions from Pen2Paper (Grand Prize, 2014, Poetry Prize 2016). She has a Ph.D. from The Catholic University of America and an MFA from George Mason University. Her publications include a scholarly book (*Grendel Recast in John Gardner's Novel and Beowulf*, 2022, Cambridge Scholars Publishing) as well as fiction and poetry (in *THEMA*, *Summerset Review*, and *Barely South Review*, among others). She teaches at Northeast State Community College in East Tennessee, where she writes and swims surrounded by mountains and books and those she loves dearly. Currently, she's working on a mystery novel and a collection of entwined short stories. Visit Sandy online at sandyhiortdahl.com.

Also published by bd-studios.com

Poetry Books

Georgia Dusk by Dudgrick Bevins & luke kurtis

Vigil by Dudgrick Bevins

Train to Providence by William Doreski & Rodger Kingston

Angkor Wat by luke kurtis

exam(i)nation by luke kurtis

(This Is Not A) Mixtape for the End of the World by Daniel M. Shapiro

The Girl Who Wasn't and Is by Anastasia Walker

Artists' Books

The Animal Book by Michael Harren

Tentative Armor by Michael Harren

Springtime in Byzantium by luke kurtis

Here Nor There by Sam Rosenthal

Just One More by Jonathan David Smyth

Architecture and Mortality by Donald Tarantino

The Male Nude by Michael Tice

Retrospective by Michael Tice

www.ingramcontent.com/pod-product-compliance
Lightning Source LLC
Chambersburg PA
CBHW041129110526
44592CB00020B/2737